香港國際詩歌之夜 *2011*
INTERNATIONAL POETRY NIGHTS IN HONG KONG

編輯 Editors

方梓勳 Gilbert C. F. Fong

陳嘉恩 Shelby K. Y. Chan

柯夏智 Lucas Klein

何潔賢 Amy Ho Kit Yin

北島 Bei Dao

宇向
Yu Xiang

目錄 Contents

理所當然

當我年事已高　有些人
依然會　千里迢迢
趕來愛我　而另一些人
會再次拋棄我

It Goes Without Saying

when I'm old   some
will still   travel miles
to love me   but others
will once again jilt me

(Translated by Fiona Sze-Lorrain)

我的房子

我有一扇門，用於提示：
當心！
你也許會迷路。
這是我的房子，狹長的
走廊，一張有風景的桌子。
一棵橘樹。一塊煤。
走廊一側是由書壘成的，
寫書的人有的死了，有的
太老了，已經不再讓人
感到危險。
我有一把椅子，有時
它會消失，如果你有誠心，
能將頭腦中其它事物
擦去，就會在我的眼中
摸到它。
我有一本《佩德羅·巴拉莫》，
裏面夾着一縷等待清洗的
頭髮。我有孤獨而
穩定的生活。
這就是我的房子。如果
你碰巧走進來，一定不是為了
我所嘮叨的這些。
你和我的房子
沒有牽連，你只是
到我這兒來

My House

I have a door, a reminder:
Be careful!
You may lose your way.
This is my house, a long narrow
hallway, a table with a view.
A tangerine tree. A piece of coal.
Stacked books form one side of the hallway.
Some of their authors are dead, some
too old, no longer exposing us
to danger.
I have a chair. Sometimes
it disappears. If you're sincere,
able to wipe other thoughts
from your mind, you'll touch it
in my eyes.
I have a copy of *Pedro Paramo*,
slotted with a strand of hair
waiting to be cleaned. I have a lonely yet
stable life.
This is my house. If
you happen to walk in, it's certainly not
for my rambling.
You and my house
are unrelated, you're just
chez moi.

(Translated by Fiona Sze-Lorrain)

街頭

順便談一談街頭，在路邊攤上
喝扎啤、剝毛豆
順便剝開緊緊跟隨我們的夏日
它會像多汁的果實，一夜間成熟
又腐爛。在夏季

順便剝開緊緊跟隨我們的往事
還有那些黑色的朗誦
簡單的愛
我們衣着簡單，用情簡單
簡單到　遇見人
就愛了

順便去愛　一個人
或另一個人，順便
把他們的悲傷帶到街頭

Street

Just talk about the street, at vendor stalls
we drink beer, peel edamame beans
Just peel open the summer tagging behind us
like a juicy fruit, it ripens overnight
and rots. In summer

just peel open the past tagging behind us
and those dark readings
A simple love
We dress simply, love simply
so simply   that we love
once we meet

Just love   someone
or anyone, just
bring their sorrows to the street

(Translated by Fiona Sze-Lorrain)

繪畫生涯

一

我得下決心去畫一些戶外景色。
就像每天上班，
必須經過那些臃腫的草莓和雞，
經過禁書、性病、傳說、
唱「回家看看」的乞丐夫妻、
篡改的歷史、塵土或尾氣般的
流竄犯，經過那些被一次一次挖開、
填平，結果再也添不平的
文化路、和平路、即時語錄、
無端的憤怒……

二

我要去畫表情和姿態，
在經期也不能停止，
以免警笛干擾筆尖的彎度和走向。
無論律法和公正如何背道而馳，
美女仍是一個活生生的奇跡，
她讓生活像顏料一樣消耗殆盡。
我的好同志，
只要我能在記憶中將你畫出來，
那麼我就永遠有事可做

三

我要畫一些靜物，
廉價賣掉，用以糊口。
我從牆上取下前輩的獎牌和勳章，
上面布滿輝煌的鏽跡，
從箱底翻出一摞紅皮證書，
再將客廳的指路明燈摔下，
為了抒情，我一遍一遍擺放它們，
這些沒落貴族般的靜物

四

沒有光線，沒有光線，
色彩像睡眠裏的對話。
夜裡，我直接將黑與白擠到畫布上。
白，塗抹鮮血，
黑，爆炸，
中間的灰調子近似於抽象的政府

五

有時，我畫赤裸裸的聲音。
當新聞聯播裏傳出風聲，
我仍聽到雙人床上的叫賣，
並在《阿姆斯特丹的河流》裏
瞬間認出——「大海的巨大徘徊」
有人說：繪畫使人墮落。
我就繼續墮落

六

如果我還有力氣，還有力氣，
我會寄一幅給你。畫面上
沒有標題也沒有簽名，
像一個又一個流亡者

A Painting Life

One

I must make up my mind to paint some outdoor scenes
like going to work every day
must pass by those puffy strawberries and chickens
pass by illegal books, sex diseases, legends
a beggar couple singing "Visit Home"
a distorted history, a dusty or tail gas-like
fugitive, those dug and re-dug
filled but never finally leveled
Cultural Street, Peace Street, improvised quotes
and undefined anger...

Two

I want to paint expression and posture
not even stopping when menstruating
lest sirens interfere with the brush's angle and direction
However law and justice may oppose
a beauty is still a living miracle
she spends away life like colors
My good comrade
as long as I can draw you in memory
I'll always have something to do

Three

I want to paint some still lifes
sell them cheap to get by
I take down my forefathers' awards and medals
stained with glorious corrosion
dig out a pile of red leather diplomas from the bottom of
    a box
then unscrew the beacon lights in the living room
For a lyrical feel, I arrange them again and again
these still lifes, like the last nobles

Four

No light, no light
colors like a sleep dialogue
At night, I squeeze black and white right onto the canvas
white smudges blood
black explodes
the gray in-between like an abstract government

Five

Sometimes I paint nude voices
When a news broadcast brings the voice of wind
I can still hear a vendor from a double bed
and in *River Amsterdam*
instantly recognize "the vast lingering of sea"
Someone says, *Drawing degenerates man*
I'll keep degenerating

Six

If I still have the strength, still have the strength
I'll send you a painting, with
no title or signature
like one exile after another

(Translated by Fiona Sze-Lorrain)

低調

一片葉子落下來
一夜之間只有一片葉子落下來
一年四季每夜都有一片葉子落下來
葉子落下來
落下來。聽不見聲音
就好像一個人獨自呆了很久，然後死去

Low Key

a leaf falls
only one leaf falls in one night
a leaf falls every night every season
leaves fall
fall, soundless
like a man who lives alone a long time, and dies

(Translated by Fiona Sze-Lorrain)

聖潔的一面

為了讓更多的陽光進來
整個上午我都在擦洗一塊玻璃

我把它擦得很乾淨
乾淨得好像沒有玻璃，好像只剩下空氣

過後我陷進沙發裡
欣賞那一方塊充足的陽光

一隻蒼蠅飛出去，撞在上面
一隻蒼蠅想飛進來，撞在上面
一些蒼蠅想飛進飛出，它們撞在上面

窗台上幾隻蒼蠅
扭動着身子在陽光中盲目地掙扎

我想我的生活和這些蒼蠅的生活沒有多大區別
我一直幻想朝向聖潔的一面

Holy Front

To let more sunlight in
I've been cleaning a glass pane the whole morning

I wipe it clean
so clean there seems no glass, just air

Then I slump into a sofa
admiring the square of bountiful sunlight

A housefly flies out, smacks into it
A housefly wants to fly in, smacks into it
Several houseflies want to fly in and out, they smack into it

On the windowsill a few flies
twitch their bodies, struggling blindly in the sun

I guess my life is no different from these flies'
I always imagine reaching a holy front

(Translated by Fiona Sze-Lorrain)

月亮

夜晚的天空布滿了月亮
只有一個月亮是明亮的
而我的月亮一定不是那個明亮的
我的月亮改變着那一個的形狀
讓它由圓變彎再由彎變圓
有時，它遮蔽它
它的四周就發出毛茸茸的光
像一圈無助的嬰兒的手

Moon

moons blanket night sky
only one moon is bright
my moon is certainly not the bright one
my moon is changing that moon's shape
let it turn from round to crescent then crescent to round
sometimes it hides it
its surroundings exude furry light
like a ring of helpless baby hands

(Translated by Fiona Sze-Lorrain)

陽光照在需要它的地方

陽光照在需要它的地方
照在向日葵和馬路上
照在更多向日葵一樣的植物上
照在更多馬路一樣的地方
在幸福與不幸的夫妻之間
在昨夜下過大雨的街上
陽光幾乎垂直照過去
照着陽台上的內褲和胸衣
洗腳房裝飾一新的門牌
照着寒冷也照着滾落的汗珠
照着八月的天空，幾乎沒有玻璃的玻璃
幾乎沒有哭泣的孩子
照到哭泣的孩子卻照不到一個人的童年
照到我眼上照不到我的手
照不到門的後面照不到偷情的戀人
陽光不在不需要它的地方

陽光從來不照在不需要它的地方
陽光照在我身上
有時它不照在我身上

Sunlight Shines Where It's Needed

sunlight shines where it's needed
shines on sunflowers and roads
shines on more sunflower-like plants
shines on more road-like places
between happy and unhappy couples
in streets with rain from last night
sunlight shines almost vertically
shines on panties and bras on the balcony
on a foot massage parlor's newly renovated door sign
shines in the cold and on falling beads of sweat
shines in an August sky, upon glass that has almost no
    glass
children who've almost no tears
shines upon weeping children but not on a childhood
shines on my eyes not on my hand
neither on the back of the door nor upon secret lovers
sunlight isn't where it isn't needed

sunlight never shines where it isn't needed
sunlight shines on my body
sometimes it doesn't shine on my body

(Translated by Fiona Sze-Lorrain)

我真的這樣想

我想擁抱你
現在，我的右手搭在我的左肩
我的左手搭在我的右肩上
我只想擁抱你，我想着
下巴就垂到胸口
現在，你就站在我面前
我多想擁抱你
迫切地緊緊地擁抱你
我這樣想
我的雙手就更緊地抱住了我的雙肩

I Really Want This

I want to hug you
now, my right hand is on my left shoulder
my left hand on my right shoulder
I just want to hug you, I want to
so my chin drops to my chest
now, you stand before me
how I long to hug you
hug you tightly, desperately
I want this
so my hands grip my shoulders even more

(Translated by Fiona Sze-Lorrain)

像人一樣

很多東西在黑暗中像人一樣
像那些坐着的站着的趴着的蹲着的蜷着的起伏的正在行走的
擺出各種姿勢的人一樣

在黑暗中所有的東西都像人，像人一樣

像人一樣驚嚇你

比如樹木座鐘馬桶掃帚空椅子有缺口的牆和石頭
還有虛掩的窗户一大堆書一灘血跡或尿跡
以及一個或兩個呆在黑暗裏的人

Like Humans

many things in the dark are like humans
like those sitting standing lying squatting coiling rolling
    now walking
humans in every pose

in the dark all things are human-like, like humans

startling you like humans do

such as trees desk clock toilet bowl broom empty chair
    chipped wall and stone
and an unlocked window a big pile of books a pool of
    blood or a urine stain
and one or two humans staying in the dark

(Translated by Fiona Sze-Lorrain)

半首詩

時不時的，我寫半首詩
我從來不打算把它們寫完
一首詩
不能帶我去死
也不能讓我以此為生
我寫它幹甚麼
一首詩
會被認識的或不相干的人拿走
被愛你的或你厭倦的人拿走
半首詩是留給自己的

Half-Poem

from time to time, I write half-poems
and never intend to finish them
a poem
can't lead me to death
and can't offer a living
why do I write it
a poem
taken away by someone you know or don't know
someone who loves or vexes you
half-poems are kept for myself

(Translated by Fiona Sze-Lorrain)

我幾乎看到滾滾塵埃

一群牲口走在柏油馬路上
我想像它們掀起滾滾塵埃

如果它們奔跑、受驚
我就能想像出更多更大的塵埃

它們是乾淨的，它們走在城市的街道上
像一群城市裏的人

它們走它們奔跑它們受驚
像烈日照耀下的人群那樣滿頭大汗

一群牲口走在城市馬路上
它們一個一個走來
它們走過我身旁

I Can Almost See the Clouds of Dust

A herd of cattle walks on a tar road
I imagine them stirring up clouds of dust

If they run, startled
I'll imagine bigger clouds of dust

They're clean, they walk on a city street
like a group of men in the city

They walk they run they're startled
like men sweating under the scorching sun

A herd of cattle walks on a city road
They come one by one
They pass by me

(Translated by Fiona Sze-Lorrain)

口袋裏的詩

一首詩放在口袋裏
如果挨着鑰匙
它會和鑰匙鏈一起發出不安的聲響
如果和硬幣在一起
也不會變成錢
它更像糖，變黏並散着甜味
如果和紙巾在一起
它會被揉皺並磨爛了邊
如果和另一首詩在一起
我想像不出怎樣
但如果它挨着避孕套
它們就形影不離
這多叫人高興
只有它們是為愛情留在了那裏

Poem in a Pocket

a poem in a pocket
if it comes with keys
it'll clatter with the key chain
if it clings onto coins
it'll not become money
more like sugar, it's sticky with a sweet scent
if it comes with a tissue paper
it'll be creased into crumples
if it finds itself with another poem
I can't imagine how
but with a condom
they'd be inseparable
what a delight
only these two stay there for love

(Translated by Fiona Sze-Lorrain)

女巫師

我高齡。能做任何人的祖母
當我右手舉起面具
左手握住心，我必定
貨真價實。擁有古老的手藝
給老鼠剃毛。把燭台弄炸
被豹子吞噬。使馬路柔腸寸斷
分崩離析那些已分崩離析的人
我懂得羞澀的儀式
會忍痛割愛。當太陽自山頭升起
照耀舞台中央的時候
我就是傳統，無人逾越
當我把祭器高舉
裡面濺出幽靈的血。是我
在人間忍受着羞辱
我是思想界最大的智慧
最小的聰明。調換左右眼
就隱藏了慈悲和邪惡
而在每一個精確的時刻
我到紡織機後配製淚水
把換來的錢攢起來
現在我打算退休
成為平凡無害的人

Sorceress

I reach a lofty age. Can be a grandmother to anyone
When my right hand lifts a mask
the left holds a heart. I'm indeed
authentic, with ancient craftmanship
to shave fur off mice. Or explode candlesticks
Devoured by leopards. I break roads
disintegrate people already disintegrated
I understand shy rituals
can bear to part with what I love. As the sun rises
lighting up the center stage
I'm the tradition, beaten by no one
As I uphold ritual vessels
ghost blood splatters. I'm the one
who bears humiliation in this world
In the realm of thoughts I'm the greatest wisdom
the pettiest cleverness. Switch both eyes
to hide mercy and evil
At each exact instant
I'll install tears behind spinning machines
accumulate the money in return
Now I plan to retire
as a harmless everyman

(Translated by Fiona Sze-Lorrain)

撒旦

一生我做一個禱告
配置我。使用我。一個完美的奴隸
但我的主仍未察覺
我變得如此具象，忠實如狗
所以我，仍被棄置
不，這也是謊言
我被逐步引入暗處
潛心追求真理

Satan

All my life I say a prayer
Configure me. Use me. A perfect slave
But my Lord still hasn't noticed
I've become so tangible, loyal as a dog
So I'm still cast aside
No, this is also a lie
I'm steadily led into the dark
deep in a gospel search

(Translated by Fiona Sze-Lorrain)

洪

我的兒女們自遠方傳來消息
他們在我之前
攜手死亡
而依然流連這世界的人們
你們還不來
咒罵我
我為你們的死已寫詩多年

在無意打開的頁面上
我的屏幕緊接着停電
於是，我的死僅有片刻的顯身：
告別之手揮動在
水平線的不平之中
你看，我的兒女們還來不及長高

他們還來不及學會簡單的生活
來不及飼養一條狗
我的兒女們還來不及譴責我的傷害
正如你們所見：多年來
我參與了人類毀滅的教育

以母親的名義生下一個孩子
給他愛和災難。我不再提出任何問題
因為上帝，不負責解答
我的上帝甚至不負責解答我的殘忍

Flood

My children bring news from afar
Before me
they hold hands with death
Those who still linger on this world
why haven't you
cursed me
I've been writing poems for your death for many years

On a random webpage
my screen blacks out
So, my death is just an instant manifestation
Hands are waving goodbye
in the tilt of the horizon
Look, my children are not yet grown-up

They've yet to learn a simple life
yet to raise a dog
My children have yet to condemn my inflictions
As you can see: for many years
I've taken part in mankind's education for destruction

given birth to a child as a mother
giving him love and disasters. I don't ask anymore
because God isn't in charge of answers
Even my God doesn't answer for my ruthlessness

(Translated by Fiona Sze-Lorrain)

我的詩

我要告訴你一件事
那是我的詩,而你正讀到它

我永遠不會飛起來,也不會離開,因為我腳踏大地,頭頂
　　天空,在為一首詩蓄備足夠的陰影

我有一把椅子,它從未發出聲響

我有另一把椅子,上面有個屁股印兒。一把沒人坐過的椅
　　子,灰塵已把屁股印埋葬

我身上有塊疤,小時候我媽打的,長大後我們「親愛的媽
媽」打的。沒人見過它,而我隨時能夠到它。在夜裏,它
是我的詩

我幾乎是由疤構成的。於是,在拐彎處,我渾身閃亮,而
　　太陽刺痛我的眼

我愛上一個藏族漢子,他糾結的長髮裏黏着虱卵和經文,
當越野車拋錨在雅江。我想着這件事的時候坐在餛飩攤
前,嘴裏含着一只被現實舐過的湯勺

如果你重溫《對她說》,請調到29分07秒,那兒有我的詩

我的生活需要一場災難,一場平息災難的災難。需要我的
　　詩

Reinaldo Arenas早已寫出我的詩句，「我一直是那個憤怒 / 而孤獨的孩子 / 總是被你侮辱 / 憤怒的孩子警告你 / 如果你虛偽地拍拍我的頭 / 我就趁機偷走你的錢包 // 我一直是那個在恐怖 / 腐敗、跳蚤 / 冒犯和罪惡面前的孩子 // 我是那個被驅逐的孩子⋯⋯」

我是那個孩子，「臉圓圓的，顯然不討人喜愛」，我喜愛
　　我的狗，但牠死了

我養的小狗一條一條死去，那是我一點一滴的冷

基督死於人，人死於他愛的事物。我該為誰哀悼

我在哀悼。別打擾我

這是我的詩，請別打擾它。

My Poem

I want to tell you something
it's my poem, you're reading it now

I'll never fly, or leave, for I stand on firm feet and look far,
    gathering shadows enough for a poem

I have a chair that makes no sound

I have another chair, with a butt print. A chair no one has
    sat in, dust has already buried the butt print

There's a scar on my body, beaten by my mother when I
was little, beaten by "Dear Mother" from our grown-up
years. No one has seen it, but I can touch it anytime. At
night, it's my poem

I'm virtually built of scars. So my body glitters at a turn,
    while the sun pierces my eyes

I'm in love with a Tibetan, his tangled long hair glued with
nits and scripture when the jeep broke down in Yajiang. I
think of this when sitting at a wonton stall, a spoon licked
by reality in my mouth

If you revisit *Hable con ella*, please rewind to 29:07, my
    poem is there

My life needs a disaster, a disaster to appease disasters.
 It needs my poem

Reinaldo Arenas already wrote my verses, *I am that angry
and lonely child of always, / that throws you the insult of
that angry child of always and warns you: / if hypocritically
you pat me on the head, / I would take the opportunity to
steal your wallet // I am that child of always / before the
panorama of imminent terror, / imminent leprosy, imminent
fleas / of offenses and the imminent crime // I am that
repulsive child…*

I'm that child, *a round face, clearly not adorable*, I like my
 dog, but it's dead

My dogs died one by one, each and every drop of my
 coldness

Christ died for man, man dies for things he loves. Who
 should I mourn

I'm mourning. Don't disturb me

This is my poem, please don't disturb it.

(Translated by Fiona Sze-Lorrain)

信

每天都有一些信在途中遺失
它與不信有關
它被風吹進樹林，吹向
林中的墳地、墓碑以及碑前的
枯枝敗葉
經過光線，它彎了一下
把死亡吹成一個美妙時刻
每天都有一個美妙的時刻
它與信有關
它落向焚燒的落葉。落在
乞丐指尖，落得下落不明
或被狗叼着，進入
動物世界
每天都有一封美妙的信，落在
雨中的路面
就像腳印
塵世被一步一步走遠

Letter *

every day some letters are lost on the way
it has to do with not believing
blown by wind into the trees, blown into
the woods, their cemeteries, their tombs and their
dead leaves
through light, it arches
blows death into a marvelous moment
every day contains a marvelous moment
it has to do with a letter
it falls onto burnt fallen leaf   falling on
beggar's fingernails, with unknown whereabouts
or bitten by a dog, entering
an animal world
every day has a marvelous letter, falling on
a road in the rain
like footprints
the world walked afar step by step

Translator's note:
* The Chinese word for "letter", xin, also means to believe.

(Translated by Fiona Sze-Lorrain)

中國70後重要詩人。曾獲「柔剛詩歌獎」（2002）、「宇龍詩歌獎」（2006）、「文化中國年度詩歌大獎」（2007）等獎項。宇向的作品「能有效挖掘自身的直覺、痛感和超驗的思維」，在海內外影響廣泛。她的作品包括詩集《哈氣》、《女巫師》，以及即將推出的詩集《我幾乎看到滾滾塵埃》。她也作為視覺藝術家參加繪畫藝術展覽。她現在居住在山東濟南。

A key figure of the post-70s Chinese poets, Yu Xiang was born in 1970 and began writing poetry in 2000. Her honors include the Rougang Poetry Prize (2002), the Yulong Poetry Prize (2006) and the Cultural China Annual Poetry Award (2007). Enigmatic and sensual, Yu Xiang's writings are immensely popular. Her works include a volume of poetry, *Exhale* (2006), a chapbook, *Sorceress* (2009), and the forthcoming collection, *I Can Almost See the Clouds of Dust*. She has also, as a visual artist, exhibited oil paintings at various venues. She currently lives in Ji'nan, the capital city of Shandong Province.

出版 Publisher
香港中文大學出版社 The Chinese University Press

封面及平面設計 Cover and Graphic Designer
朱德華 Almond Chu

製稿及分色 Art Work and Colour Separation
明星鐳射分色有限公司 Star Laser Graphic Co. Ltd.

印刷 Printer
宏亞印務有限公司 Asia One Printing Ltd.

出版日期 Date of Publication
二零一一年十月 October 2011

國際書號 ISBN
978-962-996-532-7

香港國際詩歌之夜2011主辦單位
International Poetry Nights in Hong Kong 2011 Organizers

香港中文大學東亞研究中心
Centre for East Asian Studies, The Chinese University of Hong Kong

香港城市大學人文社會科學院
College of Liberal Arts and Social Sciences, City University of Hong Kong

香港科技大學人文社會科學學院
School of Humanities and Social Science,
The Hong Kong University of Science and Technology

香港國際詩歌之夜2011協辦單位
International Poetry Nights in Hong Kong 2011 Co-organizer
木刻文化出版有限公司 MUKE Publishing Limited